AF231303

The Goat Woman of Smackover

AN ARKANSAS LEGEND

Story & Pictures by Ramona Wood

Abc Press
El Dorado, Arkansas

Wood, Ramona, 1957~
    The Goat Woman of Smackover an Arkansas Legend/by Ramona Wood ; illlustrated by Ramona Wood.~
El Dorado, AR: Abc Press, 2001, 2006, 2023
32 p. 25 cm.
Summary: The story of Rhena Miller Meyer, a once-celebrated musician who lived in a circus truck and rose above misfortune to make an impact on her community.
    1. Meyer, Rhena, 1905-1988~Juvenile literature.
    2. Arkansas~Biography~Juvenile literature.
    Title.
    ISBN 10: 0-9758622-1-9
    ISBN 13: 978-09758622-1-6   2nd printing 2006
    3rd~Print on Demand~printing 2023   Printed in the USA and other countries where ordered.

To the many Arkansans who shared their
memories and moral support. Special thanks
to Don Lambert, a pillar in the
Smackover community.

–R. W.

There was once a little girl who wanted
to be a star. Her name was Rhena (say
Rain-a) Salome Miller. She was born
in 1905 in Orwin, Pennsylvania. As a child,
she didn't want to stay home when her daddy
traveled to sell his amazing hair concoctions.
She wanted to go places and see people.

"Let me go with you!" Rhena begged when
Mr. Miller hitched up the horses for his
traveling show.

Now and then Mr. Miller took Rhena along.

"Step right up, folks! New and improved. Guaranteed to make your hair shine as never before!" Rhena's father announced to the doubtful townsfolk.

People yawned and walked away.

Then Rhena climbed onto the wagon bench. She stood tall and proud.

"Just look at her long, shiny hair," Mr. Miller cried, "She's used this fine tonic since she was a baby. Have you ever seen such beautiful hair in all your life?"

"I'll take a bottle," one lady said. Soon it was selling like hotcakes! Rhena felt like a star.

SEVEN SISTERS
SPECIAL TODAY
HAIR TONIC

And a star she became. Rhena had a gift for performing and could play any instrument she tried. Her parents made sure she went to the best music schools in the country.

She worked hard at her music lessons and as a young woman, was invited to play the piano at the world-famous Carnegie Hall in New York City.

"Where will Rhena show up next?" her fans wondered.

Rhena
the
Wonder

The next thing she knew, Rhena was boarding an ocean liner for Europe, starring in the "Greatest Show on Earth."

Rhena loved the excitement of traveling to faraway places with the Ringling Brothers, Barnum & Bailey Circus.

People watched in wonder as she played seven instruments at one time, "How DOES she do that?"

She was "Rhena, the Amazing One-Girl-Band!" It seemed like nothing could stop her now.

B ut money troubles were brewing all around the world, making it hard for people to earn a living. The big circus tour ended, leaving talented people on the streets.

Returning to the U.S., Rhena joined a small traveling circus that toured the back roads and countrysides—for pennies.

"At least I'm still making music," Rhena thought, traveling through the night to the next town. But the pennies became fewer, and the circus finally split up in Camden, Arkansas.

It was 1929, the start of the Great Depression. Rhena was very far from home and had no money. What was she to do?

CIRCUS DO
ITALY

14

Rhena and a circus partner, Charles Meyer, decided to marry and try their luck in nearby Smackover, Arkansas—a once-booming oil town.

Rhena and The Mister (as she called her much-older husband) packed up their Model-T circus truck and drove it to the middle of downtown Smackover. They set up housekeeping with their pet goats.

The townspeople weren't used to poor circus folk who raised goats in town. Some of them laughed and whispered about the "Goat Woman." Others just stared.

Rhena grew afraid of being around people. The Mister built a very high wall all around their home-on-wheels. Out front, he opened a used tire business.

Rhena rarely left her home.

Rhena no longer felt like a star. For nearly twenty years she spent the daytime hours in her little yard behind four high walls. She no longer wanted to go places and see people. In the darkness, however, the Goat Woman would slip out to walk barefoot down the streets of Smackover.

One night, Rhena took a longer walk than usual, under a full moon. She was startled by her reflection in a store window.

"This timid creature can't be me!" she thought. Rhena was tired of hiding. She wanted to be happy as she had been long ago. How could she make this happen?

The next morning, the sun beamed warmly onto Rhena as she fed her goats.

A pushy billy goat butted the other goats and then ate their food. Only Tommy, the smallest kid, wouldn't back down.

"That's right, Tommy. Stand up for yourself!"

Rhena knew that was good advice for herself, too. She had been afraid of a few thoughtless people for too long.

Bit by bit, Rhena learned she didn't have to be afraid—or lonely.

Instead of hiding when folks brought their old tires to The Mister's shop, Rhena waved.

Instead of running away when the neighbor kids giggled and peeked through the fence, she invited them in for tea.

"Play your banjo for me, pleeeease," a little girl begged. Rhena was flattered. Kids came from all over town to see where the party was.

RCUS

Rhena liked the way the children would smile, instead of laugh, at her; and she welcomed them anytime the Mister was gone. (He didn't share her new friendly attitude.) When they weren't singing, dancing, or telling stories, Rhena sent the kids with a list and a few coins to a nearby store.

When they got back, they helped Rhena make some of her favorite coconut candy.

"Guess what! A carnival's in town. Let's go!" Rhena's new friends urged one day.

"Oh, I don't know," Rhena said, shyly. But she went and rode every ride with a smile on her face.

When Rhena boarded the Ferris wheel, someone yelled, "Who let out the Goat Woman?" She just kept on smiling. She wasn't going to let someone's rudeness spoil the day.

By and by, Rhena and The Mister decided to move. They packed their belongings—goats and all—into the circus-truck and moved to Smackover Creek, three miles from town off Highway 7. Rhena didn't hide behind a tall fence anymore. She tended her goats for all to see.

Rhena made friends with her new neighbors. One lady had a mentally handicapped son and didn't go out much.

"Ora Lee," Rhena said, "make sure that boy of yours gets some of this good goat's milk."

Rhena and her trained goats began to share their music at every chance. She dropped her chores to entertain a couple of restless teenagers— or an entire troop of Camp Fire Girls. Folks lined up along the highway when Rhena put on a show. And the local country church was never the same when her gospel music rocked the rafters!

Rhena was full of surprises. One day she said to a young neighbor, "Close your eyes, dear." She gently placed a new baby goat in her arms. "He's yours."

LONDON
SPAIN
New York

Friends were there for Rhena in bad times, as well as good times. When the creek flooded in the spring, they helped the Meyers get to higher ground.

The Mister became ill and neighbors worried about him: "It's too cold in that drafty old truck." They collected some money and built them a one room house.

But Charles Meyer was very old, and he died in April of 1963.

Hard times didn't get Rhena down for long. Instead of caving in to her troubles, Rhena reached out even more. She accepted an invitation to perform with her goats on local television, her largest audience ever.

The goats shuffled into the slick-floored studio for the early morning show. One of them clambered onto the piano to stand at attention while Rhena sang an elegant solo. Then each animal sang out on cue, before joining her in a rousing polka.

Rhena never became a national celebrity, but she sparkled like a star in South Arkansas.

As the Goat Woman
grew older, folks asked why
she never went back East to
see her relatives. "I would
have to leave the goats—my
babies—and we could not
have that. They would cry
for me," she replied.

For many years, Rhena's
place was a landmark along
the Smackover highway.
Folks strained to get a
glimpse of the famous
Goat Woman out tending
her goats.

A young friend would
greet her from a passing car.
"Love life," Rhena
called out. "Live long!"
Rhena did just that.

30

BORO

**Rhena Salome Miller Meyer
died on January 21, 1988
at the age of 83.**

This circus truck that was Rhena's
home for over fifty years is housed at
the Arkansas Museum of Natural
Resources in Smackover:
AMNR.org

Part of the fascination of a legend is its curious blend of certain fact with ambiguity. This book is a composite of memories from many of Rhena's Arkansas neighbors. Her pre-Smackover days are recorded as she portrayed them to her friends.

Rhena is remembered to this day as an eccentric personality, fine musician and imaginative storyteller. Did Rhena really tour Europe with a major circus? Witnesses have seen her seven-piece musical contraption and watched her perform with astounding skill. Was she, as she has said, a cousin of the Big Band greats Les Brown and Glenn Miller? Intrigue remains in the unanswered questions.

ABOUT THE AUTHOR/ILLUSTRATOR

Ramona Karels Wood was born in Houston, Texas. She attended Ambassador College in Texas and California. She also studied at The Art Center College of Design in Pasadena and California State University of Los Angeles, receiving her B.F.A. She was a graphic designer in the Los Angeles area for eight years before returning to the South.

Her home has been El Dorado, Arkansas (a twenty-minute or so drive to the south of Smackover) since 1987. Now that their three daughters are grown, she and Steve, her husband of 38 years, cherish time with their grandkids.

Ramona writes and illustrates for children of all ages. Her work has appeared in *Pockets* magazine, *Parenting in Arkansas* magazine and various curricular publications. She has received awards for watercolor as well as line art. She is the year 2000 recipient of the National Museum of Women in the Arts scholarship (Arkansas division) for her work on *The Goat Woman of Smackover*. The grant helped make this, Ramona's first book a reality.

Since then, she has created five more books. Look for:
- *Now Caitlin Can: A donated organ helps a child get well.*
- *A Day Set Apart, Celebrating the Sabbath*
- *Kids' Book of Bible Feast Days*
- *Manners & Tips for Caring Kids*
- *Nine Ways to Win: Fruit of the Spirit Activity Book*
